CONTENTS

INTRODUCTION

Athletics is an exciting and challenging sport that consists of more than a dozen different types of event, known as disciplines. These offer a range of challenges, from the speed of sprint races or the endurance needed for marathons to explosive power in the shot put and agility in the pole vault.

Different Disciplines

Unlike some sports, athletics offers a wide range of individual disciplines that can suit people's different physiques and personalities. Events are split into two – track and field. Field events include jumping and throwing disciplines such as the triple jump and the javelin. Races held on a track, road or cross country course are called track events. Commonly held track events include two relays (4x100m and 4x400m) and two hurdles races. Occasionally, races are held at less-common distances, such as the 300m, 1000m or 2000m while the 4x800m relay and half marathon are also run.

Dawn Harper (right) lunges for the line ahead of her rivals to win the 100m women's hurdles final at the 2008 Olympic Games.

There are also two multi-discipline competitions. The men's decathlon involves ten track and field events and is held over two days. Decathletes' times, heights and distances in the events are converted to points and the athlete with the most points wins. The seven-event heptathlon replaced the pentathlon for women at the 1984 Olympics and is the leading women's multi-discipline event. Star performers, such as Carolina Klüft and Jackie Joyner-Kersee, have raised the profile of the heptathlon enormously.

Champion decathlete Roman Sebrele clears the high jump bar. The high jump is the fourth event in a decathlon between the shot put and the 400m.

A Constant Challenge

Children often take up a number of events at school and may progress to local clubs. As they grow older, athletes may specialise in a single discipline, enjoying the thrill of competing in local, regional or national competitions and receiving expert coaching. A handful of elite athletes will turn professional, earning money from funding, sponsorship, appearance fees and prizes. After their competitive career is over, some athletes become officials, coaches, or take part in events for veterans.

MAD FACT

Bob Mathias was just 17 years old when he won the decathlon at the 1948 Olympics. He had taken up the event only a few months beforehand.

THEN AND NOW

Running, throwing and jumping disciplines are amongst the oldest sporting events. Artefacts depicting races, spear or javelin throwing, and high and long jumpers have been found in ancient Egypt and Iraq. Some date back to about 5,000 years ago.

The Ancient Olympics

A number of 'games' – events involving religious ceremonies and athletics events – became popular in ancient Greece about 3,000 years ago. The games at Olympia began in 776 BCE and emerged as the most important, lasting for more than 1,200 years.

MAD FACT

At the ancient Olympics, winning athletes received a *kotinos* (a crown of olive leaves) but often returned to a hero's welcome and prizes at home.

Athletics Revival

In the nineteenth century, many athletics events became more organised as interest in the sport grew. The oldest surviving athletics organisation, the Amateur Athletic Association (AAA) was founded in England in 1880. Later, in 1896, a revival of the ancient Greek Olympics was held in Athens. Athletics received a double boost in 1912, with a well-organised Olympics in Stockholm, Sweden, that helped to establish the competition, and form the International Amateur Athletic Federation (IAAF).

Russia's Gulnara Galkina-Samitova leads the field on the way to winning the women's 3000m steeplechase at the 2008 Olympics. This was the first time this race was held at an Olympics, after making its debut at the World Athletics Championships in 2005.

...Jesse Owens?

America's Jesse Owens came to prominence when he equalled the 100 yard (91m) world record while still at high school. In May 1935, he equalled the record again and broke three other world records (for the long jump, the 220 yard sprint (201m) and 220 yard hurdles) — all in the space of 45 minutes! At the 1936 Olympic Games, Owens was the undoubted star, as he took part in four events (100m, 200m, long jump and 4x400m relay) and won gold in all of them. In the long jump, after struggling to qualify for the final, he produced three of the longest jumps in the competion. Owens returned to the United States where he is remembered as one of the finest athletes of all time.

Owens leaps long and high as he competes in the long jump competition at the 1936 Olympic Games.

Great Changes

Athletics has changed hugely since the Olympics of the early twentieth century. Women athletes were first allowed to compete at the 1924 Olympics and then only in six events. Today, male and female athletes take part in almost all events. As athletes have become full-time and have taken advantage of the latest research and technology in training and sports science, world records have tumbled. For example, the women's marathon world record set by Paula Radcliffe in 2005 was a staggering one hour and 12 minutes faster than the record set by Dale Grieg in 1964.

MAD FACT

When competing at the 1936 Olympics, track sprinters, including Jesse Owens, had to dig small holes in the track to get a foothold because there were no starting blocks.

AIM OF THE SPORT

The motto of the modern Olympic Games is 'Citius, Altius, Fortius', meaning 'Faster, Higher, Stronger'. Athletics is all about running faster, jumping higher or longer or throwing greater distances than before, as well as performing better than other athletes.

Finishing First

The aim of most events seems simple – to cross the line first or to jump or throw further than others – but there are rules attached to what makes a win. Throwers have to stay within their throwing area, for example. Athletes in some races, such as the 100m, 200m, 400m and hurdles races, have to stay in their lane. Running out of their lane, even if it is just a single step in another lane, leads to disqualification. To win any track race, an athlete's torso or trunk has to break the finish line before his or her opponents'.

> **MAD ///// FACT**
>
> Heike Drechsler's record-breaking 7.63m long jump in 1992 was disallowed as the wind assistance was 2.1m/s, which is 0.1 m/s over the maximum allowed.

Personal Bests

Athletes aim to reach peak condition to coincide with major championships. Most focus on their own performances, knowing they cannot influence how their opponents perform. That said, they hope to outperform their rivals or strive to record a personal best (PB) – their best time, height or distance in an event.

Cuba's Dayron Robles (right) clears the last hurdle on his way to winning the 110m hurdles final at the 2008 Olympics.

?

Who is...

...Yelena Isinbayeva?

One of the greatest record-breakers of recent years, Yelena Isinbayeva took up the pole vault in 1997 after a career in gymnastics. The following year, she won gold at the World Youth Games. After winning the World Junior Championships in 2000, Isinbayeva broke the world outdoor record in 2003 with a vault of 4.82m. It was the first of 16 world records to be broken outdoors by the Russian. At the 2008 Olympics, her vault of 5.05m won Isinbayeva her second Olympic gold. Despite fierce competition, she continues to dominate the sport, winning the World Indoor Championships in 2008, and setting a new indoor world record in February 2009.

Yelena Isinbayeva performs at an indoor meeting in 2009. In February that year, she became the first woman to clear 5 metres indoors.

World Records

World records (WR) are the best performance ever in an event. They have to be checked and approved by the IAAF before they can be made official. For a world record to count, certain rules have to be followed. For example, in the jump events and in the 100m and 200m sprints, wind assistance must be no more than 2m/s for a world record to apply. This has led to some disappointed athletes, including Obadele Thompson. In 1996, he ran the 100m in a scorching 9.69 seconds, but with wind assistance of 5m/s, so the record didn't stand.

MAD //// FACT

Ivan Pedrosa's 1995 record-breaking 8.96m long jump appeared to be fine, with the wind assistance at 1.2m/s. It was then discovered that someone had been standing in front of the wind gauge, and this had stopped the instrument from making an accurate measurement.

THE STADIUM AND OFFICIALS

With the exception of events such as marathons, racewalking and cross country races, all events take place in outdoor stadiums. Most, but not all, events can also be held in indoor venues.

Track and Field

An outdoor track is oval in shape and usually 400m long. It consists of eight or more lanes, each 1.22m wide. Amateur tracks may be marked out on a grass field but at major stadiums, tracks are made from high-tech materials with a surface that offers the ideal balance of grip and pace for athletes. While the finish line is set at the end of the home straight, starting points for races vary. In events such as the 200m and 400m sprints, where athletes have to stay in their lanes, the runners start from a staggered position around the track bend. This is so that every athlete completes the same distance.

Throwing events tend to take place in the oval inside the track. Competitors in the hammer and discus perform inside a safety cage to protect spectators and officials against miss-throws. The triple jump and long jump may share a single runway and long landing pit filled with sand, while the pole vault and high jump tend to have their own dedicated areas, often inside one of the track bends.

A typical athletics track includes:	*3) javelin runway*	*7) pole vault area*
1) finish line	*4) shot put throwing sector*	*8) staggered start for 200m*
2) long jump and triple jump sandpit	*5) hammer and discus area*	*9) 100m start*
	6) high jump arena	*10) 110m hurdles start*

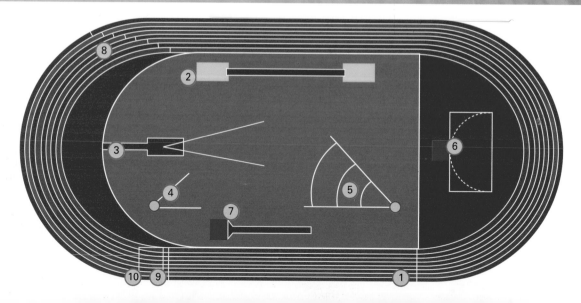

Indoor Venues

Indoor tracks vary in size but most are 200m long and four or six lanes wide. The outside lanes are often banked (sloped inwards) to help runners competing in races in which they must stay in lane. Adjustments are made to some events held indoors. For example, 100m sprinters run 60m on a straight, cutting through the middle of the oval, while the 400m hurdles and 3000m steeplechase are rarely run indoors. Many indoor venues allow most of the field events to take place. At the occasional indoor meeting, male decathletes compete in an indoor heptathlon (60m sprint, long jump, shot put, high jump, 60m hurdles, pole vault and 1000m).

The lanes of a running track are clearly marked with numbers, for races in which the athletes have to stay in lane at all times.

Officials

There are usually dozens of officials and stewards at an athletics meeting. They perform a range of tasks, from guiding athletes out for their event at the right time to measuring the length of jumps and throws. An official will signal either a white flag for a legal jump or throw, or a red flag if the attempt breaks the rules in some way. There are also timekeepers and starters for events, and officias who check on an athlete's equipment and clothing and judge on close finishes and other disputes.

A long jump attempt by Paralympic athlete Xavier le Draollec of France receives a red flag from an official. Le Draollec received three red flagged jumps during the 2008 Paralympic Games, which put him out of the competition.

SPRINTS

The most explosive events in track athletics are the sprints, from 60m indoor events to 400m – a full lap of the track. Sprinting requires fast reactions, power to accelerate rapidly and great strength and technique to maintain maximum speed.

Starter's Orders

All sprints start with an official, called the starter, asking the sprinters to get 'on their marks'. The competitors get into their starting blocks, with fingers placed on the track behind the start line and with one knee on the ground. The starter then asks the sprinters to 'set'. The athletes raise their hips above their shoulders and are primed for the firing of the starter's gun. As it fires, the sprinters explode out of their starting blocks, driving forwards with short but strong strides to build up speed. As they accelerate to their maximum speed, their body uncurls to an upright position within 20–30 metres.

False Starts

A false start is when a sprinter leaves his or her blocks before the starter's gun has fired. In the past, this was judged by the human eye, but today it is done electronically. In professional athletics, the starting blocks have footpad sensors linked to an electronic timing system. These measure the pressure of the sprinter's feet on the blocks and can determine whether he or she has an illegal reaction time. Within seconds of a false start, the starter fires the gun again and the sprinters regroup for a second start. If any athlete is responsible for another false start, he or she will be disqualified.

Female athletes power out of the blocks during a heat of the 100m competition at the 2003 World Athletics Championships. Runners competed in heats, quarter- and semi-finals, and the final, which was won by Torri Edwards of the United States in a time of 10.93 seconds.

200m and 400m

Sprinters in the 200m and 400m have to run at top speed around the track's bends. They tend to run towards the inside of their lane and lean inwards to counteract the forces pushing them outwards. They run the last portion of the race down the home straight, having to fight off fatigue and trying to maintain a relaxed running style. It is here that an athlete's stamina and strength training become especially important. Winners are often those who are able to maintain their form through the finishing line.

Who is...

...Usain Bolt?

In 2002, at just 15 years of age, Usain Bolt became the youngest World Junior Champion to win the 200m. Although injuries restricted his development, he won silver in the 100m and 200m at the 2007 World Championships and then entered the 2008 Olympics as favourite for both the 100m and 200m. Bolt destroyed the rest of the 100m field with a dazzling display, setting a new world record of 9.69 seconds. He followed up with a 200m win in 19.30 seconds, beating Michael Johnson's previous world record of 19.32 seconds. Bolt was also part of the Jamaican 4x100m relay team that won Olympic gold and smashed the world record in the process.

Usain Bolt crosses the line to win the 100m final of the 2008 Olympics in the record-breaking time of 9.69 seconds.

HURDLES AND RELAYS

Hurdles events take place over 60m indoors or over 100m or 110m and 400m outdoors. Relays feature teams of four athletes who all run the same distance (either 100m or 400m), passing a baton between runners.

Hurdles Races

The 100m hurdles for women and the 110m hurdles for men both feature ten hurdles, placed at regular intervals down each lane of the track. Athletes throw their front leg over the hurdle and then bend their trailing leg up and out to clear the hurdle. Hurdlers are allowed to knock over hurdles without being disqualified, but striking a hurdle usually leads to a loss of speed and balance.

The 400m hurdles is one of the toughest tests on the track. Runners have to maintain a regular stride pattern between the ten hurdles so that they clear each one smoothly. As fatigue mounts, some hurdlers are forced to alter their stride length or to take shuffling steps to get into a position to clear the last few hurdles.

Lolo Jones was the clear leader of the 2008 Olympics 100m hurdles final until she clipped the second from last hurdle. Stumbling and losing speed, she finished the race in seventh place.

Two of Saudi Arabia's 4x400m relay team exchange the baton as they run towards victory at the 2006 Asian Games. To achieve a slick baton changeover, the next runner needs to be building up speed as he receives the baton.

4x100m Relay

In the 4x100m, a team stays in its lane throughout the race. The baton is switched between runners in a 20m stretch of track called the changeover zone. As the baton holder approaches, the receiver builds up speed. The baton is swept up or down into the next sprinter's trailing hand. The team is disqualified if the exchange is not completed inside the changeover zone. Smooth baton changeovers that do not impede either runner's speed are crucial to success. A clumsy or slow changeover or dropped baton can mean disaster. At the 2005 World Athletics Championships, the US team was favourite partly because it included world 100m and 200m champion, Justin Gatlin. In a heat, though, the baton was dropped and the team failed to make the final.

4x400m Relay

The 4x400m starts with the lead-off runners (the first in each team) running a regular 400m lap. The only difference is that their starting positions are more staggered than usual. The second-leg runners stay in lane and the changeover is similar to that of the 4x100m. As they round the first bend, runners can break and move to the inside lane. The changeovers to the third and the fourth runners can involve barging and jostling as the receivers line up across the track waiting for the baton.

S T A T A T T A C K			
World Records Over 400m in seconds			
	400m	**4x100m**	**Hurdles**
Men	43.18	37.10	46.78
Women	47.60	41.37	52.34

MIDDLE AND LONG DISTANCE EVENTS

Some of the most epic battles on the track have occurred in middle (800m-3000m) and long distance (5000m and above) running. Apart from consistent speed throughout a race, competitors need tactical awareness and often the ability to sprint at the finish.

Race Start

The shortest middle distance event, the 800m, has a staggered start, but runners do not have to stay in lane for the whole race – they can break towards the inside lane after 100m. Runners in a 1500m race start along a curved line on the far side of the track. Runners in a 5000m and 10,000m race start in a straight line across the track and can break immediately.

Race Tactics

Once a race is underway, tactics are vital. Some races are fast right from the start. Runners who lack a notable sprint finish or are feeling in prime form may lead from the front, hoping to break the rest of the field with fast laps. In contrast, some races are slower and more cagey, with no runner prepared to take the lead. These races can suit runners who wish to make a break in the final laps or have a powerful sprint finish.

Kelly Holmes celebrates as she wins the 1500m race to add to her 800m gold at the 2004 Olympics. Holmes became the first British woman to win two gold medals in athletics at a single Olympics.

By the time the bell sounds, indicating runners have begun the last lap, the pace tends to wind up no matter the race distance. As runners fight fatigue and try to accelerate, they stay aware of who they regard as the biggest threat and strive not to become boxed in. This is where they are stuck on the inside bend behind and inside other runners, preventing them from overtaking.

Close Finishes

Many races end in close finishes. In the men's 800m final at the 2007 World Championships, the top eight runners all finished within half a second of each other. One of the closest-ever finishes in long distance running occurred in 2000 when, after running the 10,000m, Haile Gebrselassie and Paul Tergat were separated by only 0.009 seconds, with Gerbrselassie emerging as the winner.

Doubling Up

A small number of highly talented athletes have attempted to double up at a major championship, running two middle or long distance events. Doubling up in the 800 and 1500m or the 5,000m and 10,000m is most commonly attempted, although at the 1983 World Championships, Czechoslovakia's Jarmila Kratochvilová doubled up in the 400m and 800m. She managed to win them both. With heats having to be run at a major championship to qualify for the final race, doubling up is the ultimate test of a middle or long distance athlete's powers of recovery. Two of the most notable double victories include Kelly Holmes's (800m and 1500m) at the 2004 Olympics and Tirunesh Dibaba's (5000m and 10,000m) at the 2005 World Championships.

Who is...

...Kenenisa Bekele?

Ethiopia's Kenenise Bekele won the junior competition of the IAAF World Cross Country Championship in 2001 and has since gone on to win the men's 12km competition a record six times. On the track, his relentless running style and incredibly fast sprint finish, even at the end of a gruelling race, have seen him win three World Championship titles and two Olympic 10,000m gold medals, an Olympic gold in the 5,000m and a World Indoor 3000m title.

Kenenisa Bekele (left) races against his younger brother, Tariku, at the Shanghai Golden Grand Prix in China in 2005. At the 2008 Olympics, Kenenisa Bekele shattered the Olympic 5000m record by almost eight seconds.

MARATHONS AND RACEWALKING

The ultimate long distance running challenge, the marathon, joins racewalking to form the two greatest tests of endurance at an athletics event.

The Marathon

The marathon's strange distance stems from the 1908 Olympics where, legend has it, the finish line was moved to afford the British royal family a better view of the action. The marathon challenges athletes to complete 42.195km, running at consistently high speeds. Elite runners complete a marathon in just over two hours and make use of feeding stations along the course to replenish lost fluids and nutrients. City marathons such as those held in London, Berlin and New York attract thousands of runners, many of whom are amateurs who run for charity. At major competitions, the marathon ends with a final lap around the track used to hold the other events of the competition.

Paula Radcliffe leads from the front to win the 2008 New York City Marathon. It was the third time she had won the event.

Racewalking

The longest event at many championships is the men's 50km racewalk. There are also 20km races for both men and women. Racewalkers take 3 or 3.5 steps every second (in comparison, a 100m runner takes 4.5 steps per second but only for 10 seconds). They race under strict rules. For example, part of one foot must always be in contact with the ground, meaning that the front foot must be touching the ground before the rear foot can be completely lifted. Judges line a racewalking course and warn runners of infringements by raising a yellow paddle. If three judges award red cards to the same racewalker, they are disqualified. At the 2008 Olympics, five athletes were disqualified from the Men's 50km and three from the women's 20km race.

Stamina and Cadence

Marathon runners and racewalkers have incredible stamina. At an international-level marathon, athletes complete each kilometre in or under three minutes.

Cadence is the number of steps taken in a set period of time. To compete at the highest level, racewalkers must maintain the cadence of a 400m runner but for hours at a time. This requires vast amounts of stamina, concentration and technical excellence.

MAD //// //// FACT

When racewalker Jefferson Perez won Ecuador's first ever Olympic medal in 1996, his grateful country awarded him a lifetime's free supply of yoghurt!

Eddy Riva (left) of France and Antonio Pereira cool themselves with water as they take part in the gruelling 50km racewalk at the 2007 World Championships. Australia's Nathan Deakes won the race in a time of 3 hours, 43 minutes and 53 seconds.

STEEPLECHASE AND CROSS-COUNTRY

Long and middle distance runners sometimes compete in two further disciplines that test their stamina, technique and concentration – steeplechase and cross country races.

The 3000m Steeplechase

Derived from horseracing over jumps, a steeplechase is a fast middle-distance race. It is usually run over 3,000m, although junior athletes may race over shorter distances. Athletes have to clear track-wide barriers 28 times and a large water jump seven times throughout the race. The barriers and the water jump reward those athletes who have a better hurdling technique. Such athletes are less likely to lose momentum when hurdling or be involved in a dramatic fall, such as Marta Dominguez's tumble in the 2008 Olympics women's steeplechase final – she fell with just 250m left to run.

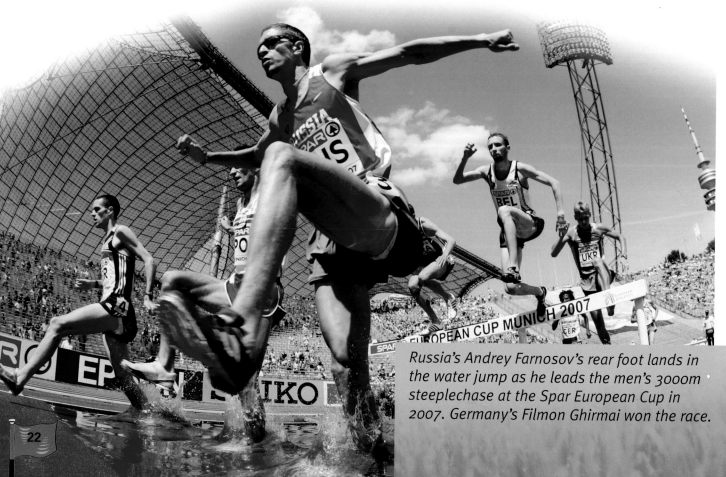

Russia's Andrey Farnosov's rear foot lands in the water jump as he leads the men's 3000m steeplechase at the Spar European Cup in 2007. Germany's Filmon Ghirmai won the race.

Cross Country

Cross-country races take place on a course plotted on grass, tracks, fields, dips and hills. Popular at amateur level, events vary in distance and include competitions for individual runners and teams, sometimes with individual and team competitions in the same race. In team events, athletes are awarded points depending on where they finish. The further down the field they finish, the more points they accumulate. The winning team is the one with the fewest points. In the IAAF competition (see below), teams of nine runners each compete, with their six best-placed finishers counting towards their tally.

World Cross Country

While many countries have their own national cross-country competitions, the leading event is the IAAF World Cross Country Championships, which began in 1973. Held every year, they include a 12km course race for men and an 8km course for women. The field is usually very competitive, with top runners who may normally compete in separate events, such as the marathon or 10,000m, racing for first place. In recent decades, African runners have dominated with Kenya's Paul Tergat winning the men's event five times in a row and Tirunesh Dibaba winning three of the last five women's titles.

Two Ethiopian runners sandwich Australia's Benita Johnson during the 2004 IAAF World Cross Country Championships. Johnson won the 8km race in a time of 27 minutes and 17 seconds.

LONG AND TRIPLE JUMP

The long jump and triple jump are all about obtaining maximum distance. In both events, athletes take a long run up along a strip of track, called the runway, before leaping into a sandpit.

Jump Rules

Both long jumpers and triple jumpers aim to hit the take-off board but without touching a strip of modelling clay attached to the edge of it. Officials will signal a 'no jump' if any mark is made on the clay. A jump is measured from the edge of the take-off board to the closest mark made by the jumper in the sand. This is why jumpers aim to get their legs and body down and forward into the sand on landing and avoid sticking their hands out and behind themselves.

STAT ATTACK

Longest Running Long Jump Records

1935 Jesse Owens (8.13m) 25 years

1968 Bob Beamon (8.90m) 23 years

1991 Mike Powell (8.95m) 18 years

Jackie Edwards jumps at the Commonwealth Games in 2006. Her body, legs and arms are all thrust forward to gain maximum distance before touching the sand.

5   6

The Triple Jump

An extremely technical event, the triple jump requires speed, poise and balance. The athlete sprints along the runway, takes off and lands on the same foot to perform the hop phase, then takes as long a step as possible before leaping into the sandpit. Keeping each movement as smooth as possible helps reduce the loss of speed and momentum that occurs through the sequence of moves. Triple jumpers also aim for rhythm in their movements to gain maximum distance.

Who is...
Jonathan Edwards?

Jonathan Edwards is the world record holder in the triple jump, a record he has held since 1995 when he jumped 18.29m at the European Cup. At that competition, he jumped 18.16m in a previous round before breaking the world record again 20 minutes later. A gold medal at the 2000 Olympics to add to his World Championship, European Championship, Commonwealth Games and six European cup victories, made him the leading triple jumper of his era. He retired in 2003, and is now a member of the organising committee for the 2012 London Olympics.

Jonathan Edwards competes in the 2001 World Championships, where he won another gold medal to add to his world record and Olympic gold.

The Long Jump

Long jumpers are given a set number of attempts to jump. They start at the far end of the runway having marked out their run-up – usually between 20 and 22 strides. Building as much speed as possible on the runway, they leap off the take-off board, getting their legs ahead of their body, and aiming to clear as much sand as possible before landing. Sprinting speed is essential, which is why successful long jumpers, such as Carl Lewis, Heike Dreschler and Jackie Joyner-Kersee were also world-class sprinters. Drechsler won Olympic medals in the 100m and 200m and, at the 2000 Games, became the oldest female long jump winner at the age of 35.

MAD FACT

At 2.03m, Brazilian triple jumper, Jadel Gregório, is one of the world's tallest. At the 2008 Beijing Olympics, a special extension to his bed had to be built.

HIGH JUMP AND POLE VAULT

In the high jump and pole vault competitors have to clear a bar that sits on two upright supporting poles. Athletes are allowed to touch the bar and make it wobble, but it is not allowed to fall off its supports.

High Jump

The high jump arena consists of a large area, called the high jump runway, and the high jump itself. The bar rests on upright poles approximately 4 metres apart with a crash mat behind. In most competitions, jumpers are given up to 90 seconds to complete each of their jumps. Jumpers approach the bar in a curving run, using a bouncy stride on the balls of their feet. They drive upwards off one foot and travel head first over the bar, arching their back and pulling up their feet to clear it. Great champions over the years include Iolanda Bala, who in the 1950s and 1960s was unbeaten in 140 competitions. In men's high jumping, Cuba's Javier Sotomayor stands out. He is the current world record holder with a jump of 2.45m.

Pole Vault

Competitors in the pole vault use a flexible pole, usually 4–5m long, which bends under their weight and then recoils, sending them upwards, to clear the pole with their arms and legs. After their run-up, vaulters plant their pole in a slot known as the vaulting box. As they spring up, they turn their hips to reach a vertical position, upside-down with their legs extended. They push off the pole,

Croatia's Blanka Vlašić arches her back and then hitches up her feet and legs on her way to clearing the bar at the 2008 Olympics.

STAT ATTACK

Selected Men's Pole Vault World Record Progression

1912	4.02m	Daniel Conaselli
1937	4.54m	Bill Sefton
1963	5.00m	Brian Sternberg
1966	5.32m	Bob Seagren
1972	5.51m	Kjell Isaksson
1981	5.80m	Thierry Vigneron
1985	6.00m	Sergey Bubka
1994	6.14m	Sergey Bubka

arch their body and aim to clear the bar with their arms and legs. As they fall, they twist in order to land on their back on the crash mat below. With competition heights typically around 5 metres for women and 6 metres for men, the action is amongst the most spectacular in athletics.

In Competition

As jumpers or vaulters clear a height, the bar is raised, usually in units of centimetres. Athletes who fail to clear a given height three times in a row exit the competition. The winner is the athlete who completes a jump or vault of a greater height than their rivals. If two or more athletes have achieved the same height, the competitor who has the least number of failures, either at the final height or in the competition overall, is the winner. At the 2008 Olympics, gold-medal prospect Blanka Vlašić and Belgium's Tia Hellebaut both cleared 2.05m, but Hellebaut won as she had taken only one attempt at 2.05m to Vlašić's two.

Steve Fritz makes a successful vault at the World Athletics Championships. He arches his back and times the letting-go of his pole to clear the bar.

SHOT PUT AND DISCUS

In shot put and discus, athletes are allowed a set number of attempts to throw as far as possible. The shot or discus has to land in a marked-out arc, called the landing sector or area.

Throwing Circles

Both the discus and the shot are thrown from a throwing circle. The discus circle is 2.5m in diameter and has a small raised lip around its edge. The shot put circle is 2.135m and has a curved bar, 10cm high, at the front called the stopboard. Shot putters can brace their front feet against this board to aid their throw and to stop themselves from toppling over after they release the shot. In both events, athletes must leave the throwing circle from the rear half. If they step out at the front of the circle, their throw is invalid.

Valerie Vili drives up just before releasing the shot put at the 2006 IAAF World Cup in Athens. Vili, a New Zealander, won the shot put competition at the 2008 Olympics .

Putting the Shot

The shot is a solid metal ball weighing 7.26 kilograms for men and 4 kilograms for women. The shot is cradled in the neck using the fingers. Shot putters can use the rotational method, turning around one of their feet, which acts as a pivot, or they can use the O'Brien or linear technique. This is named after Parry O'Brien who used the technique to break the world record 16 times throughout his career. Using the linear technique, the thrower leans out of the back of the circle, makes a low hop across the circle and drives from a low position to a high one, extending the throwing arm.

MAD /// /// FACT

American discus thrower Al Oerter is the only field athlete to have won his event in four consecutive Olympics – 1956, 1960, 1964 and 1968.

Roman Sebrle of the Czech Republic completes a throw at the 2008 Olympics. He releases the discus with his fingers pressing on its edge to send it spinning away smoothly.

The Discus

Discus throwers need expert timing, balance and control of their body throughout their throw. They begin each throw by making preliminary swings of the discus back and forth to build rhythm. They then turn powerfully as they cross the circle with the discus sent on as wide and as powerful a swing as possible before releasing it. Throwers are front-on as their throwing arms swing from low to high before releasing the discus. A good release sends the discus spinning smoothly through the air. The women's world record of 76.80 metres by Gabrielle Reinsch is further than the men's. This is because the women's discus weighs a kilogram less than the men's. Both the men's and women's discuses are 220mm in diameter.

HAMMER AND JAVELIN

Although quite different in technique, both hammer and javelin throwers rely on timing, power and an ideal release angle to send their projectile huge distances.

The Hammer

The hammer is a 1.2-metre long chain with a handle at one end and a metal ball on the other. The men's hammer weighs 7.26 kilograms and the women's 4 kilograms. It is thrown from a 2.1m wide circle surrounded at the back and sides by a safety cage. Throwers start at the back of the circle with preliminary swings of the hammer to lift it off the ground. They then build up power and momentum with three or four complete turns of their body as neat footwork takes them to the front of the circle. The speed of the hammer increases through these turns so that as they release the hammer over their left shoulder. In 1978, West Germany's Karl-Hans Riehm broke the 80-metre mark. Eight years later, Yuriy Sedekh of the Soviet Union threw a massive 86.74m, a world record which still stands.

Ivan Tsikhan of Belarus competes at the 2007 World Championships on his way to winning the gold medal. He increases the speed of the hammer during the preliminary swings before winding up his body, turning across the circle and releasing the hammer.

Who is...

...Barbora Špotáková?

Czech javelin thrower Barbora Špotáková began her athletics career as a promising heptathlete, coming fourth in the 2000 World Junior Championships. After switching solely to the javelin, improvement came slowly at first, but in 2006, Špotáková won second place at the European Championship. The next year, she won the World Championship and, in 2008, claimed Olympic gold. Two months after her Olympic success, at the IAAF World Athletics Final, Špotáková broke the world record by 58cm with a huge throw of 72.28m.

The Javelin

The javelin event takes place on a long strip, known as the runway, which ends with the scratch line. If athletes cross this line, their throw is illegal. Throwers start with the javelin held just above shoulder height and roughly parallel with the ground. They move forward on the runway, building speed, before using a crossover stride to turn side-on and draw back the javelin. As they hit their delivery stride, they brace their front leg and pull the javelin through as they turn to face forwards. They then release it as their throwing arm passes by the side of their head. Once the javelin is released, its point must touch the ground first. As athletes improved their technique, throws increased in length and even started to threaten spectators at some meetings. As a result, the javelins were re-designed, moving their centre of gravity forwards to reduce their likely distance and to increase the likelihood of point-first landings.

Barbora Špotáková draws back the javelin before unleashing a powerful throw at the 2007 World Athletics Championships. She won the event, with a throw of 67.07m.

IN TRAINING

Athletes put in thousands of hours' training to improve their strength, speed, endurance and the techniques demanded by their discipline. They work closely with a coach and have to manage all aspects of their lifestyle carefully.

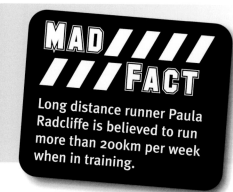

MAD //// //// FACT

Long distance runner Paula Radcliffe is believed to run more than 200km per week when in training.

In Training

A training session may involve building strength and power either in the gym or via other exercises, as well as honing techniques under the eyes of a coach. Flexibility is vital so most athletes, from sprinters to pole vaulters, do flexibility exercises in training, as well as extensive warm up exercises and stretches before competition. Training programmes are often designed to build peak performance in time for major events.

Discipline and Setbacks

Athletes have to be disciplined to avoid things that could impact on their training. They eat healthily, following advice from nutritionists, and know that even a few missed training sessions can have a dramatic impact on their performance. An athlete is most likely to turn to his or her coach, friends and family, after suffering a desperate defeat or a frustrating injury. Many champion athletes emerge stronger for the setbacks they experience and return to competition faster and fitter. For example,

Canadian high jumper Nicole Forrester warms up before her event at the Commonwealth Games. Many athletes show incredible levels of flexibility.

American athlete Brian Clay was unable to complete the decathlon at the 2007 World Championships due to a thigh muscle injury, but won the 2008 Olympic gold medal.

Performance-enhancing Drugs

Despite significant health risks, possible punishments and the stigma of being labelled a drugs cheat, some athletes use drugs to try to give them the edge. The list of banned substances includes anabolic steroids, which promote muscle growth, and EPO (erythropoietin), which increases the amount of oxygen that red blood cells carry around the body. It is the responsibility of an athlete and his or her coach to avoid banned substances. Top athletes are tested for banned drugs frequently and may face a ban if they test positive. In 2004, the world 400m champion, Jerome Young, was banned for life after being found guilty of using EPO. Heptathlete Lyudmila Blonska, a silver medallist at the 2008 Olympics, suffered the same fate after she tested positive for a banned steroid.

MAD FACT

In 2007, while training in South Africa, champion decathlete Roman Sebrle was hit by a wayward javelin which sank 12cm into his arm. He recovered to win the 2007 World Championships.

Chinese 110m hurdles star Liu Xiang works hard during weights training. Months earlier he had endured heartbreak at the Olympics when an injury meant that he had to miss the event in front of his home crowd.

BIG COMPETITIONS

Top athletes compete in a wide range of meetings and championships and many of these competitions are events for individual athletes. However, in some, such as the Olympic Games, athletes compete as part of their national team.

Grand Prix and Golden League

The biggest and most prestigious athletics events include Grand Prix meetings and the IAAF Golden League. The latter ran from 1998 until 2009 and was made up of six or seven meetings. Athletes who won their events at every meeting shared a huge prize – either US$1 million or 40kg of gold bars. In most seasons, several athletes shared the prize, but in 2008, 800m runner Pamela Jelimo won the whole lot! In 2010, the Golden League was replaced by the Diamond League. This features about 12 meetings per season.

A delighted Pamela Jelimo poses with two of the solid gold bars that were her prize for winning the Golden League competition in 2008.

World Tour and Final

Grand Prix and Diamond League meetings are also part of the World Tour – 25 meetings in which the top-placed athletes in each event receive points. For example, in 2008, first place at a Golden League meeting earned an athlete 20 points, while first place at a lower-standard meeting scored six points. Athletes' five best points performances are added up and the top competitors in each event are invited to a World Final. At the 2008 World Final in Stuttgart, Sanya Richards won the women's 200m and 400m and Vadims Vasielevskis made the longest throw of the year (89.65m) in the javelin.

National Championships

Many countries have national championships, with some having separate indoor and outdoor events at different times of the year. Some, such as the French National Championship, invite athletes from overseas, too. Sometimes, they are used as trials for forthcoming events. The US Trials is considered one of the toughest of all national competitions, especially in an Olympic year. In 2008, athletes who peaked at the trials included Tyson Gay in the 100m and Jennifer Stuczynski in the pole vault, both of whom set US records.

Poland's Szymon Ziolkowski competes in the men's hammer throw at the IAAF Japan Grand Prix in Osaka, in 2006.

CONTINENTAL COMPETITIONS

Although national meetings often attract an excellent field of athletes, the competition intensifies at an international meeting, in which the world's best athletes take part.

The European Championships

The European Championships have been held once every four years, with several exceptions, since 1934. After the 2010 championships in Barcelona, they will be held every two years. Although the championships have never been held in Britain, British athletes come third in the all-time medal list behind Russia and East Germany. Featuring the cream of European athletes, the standard at the European Championships can be extremely high. For example, at the 1986 championships in Stuttgart, Yuriy Sedykh threw 86.74m in the hammer, a world record yet to be equalled. At the 2006 championship in Gothenburg, Francis Obikwelu, running for Portugal, won the men's 100m and 200m. There was also a tie in the 100m hurdles. Kirsten Bolm and Derval O'Rourke both finished in 12.72 seconds.

The 4x400m relay teams from the Bahamas and the USA lie neck and neck as they exchange their batons during a race at the 2007 Pan-American Games.

Multi-Sport Competitions

Apart from the Olympics, there are a number of international competitions featuring a range of sports in which athletics plays an important part. The Commonwealth Games is held once every four years for countries that were former colonies of or linked to Great Britain. The 2006 competition held in Australia featured competitors from 71 countries. The 2014 Games is set for the Scottish city of Glasgow. The Asian Games is Asia's leading sports competition and was held in Qatar in 2006. Both the Commonwealth Games and the Asian Games may have strong fields in some events, but with no United States or European nations, they suffer from weak fields in others. For example, at the 2006 Games, Chinese hammer thrower Zhang Wenxiu won the women's competition 9.02 metres ahead of second place.

Pan-American Games

The Pan-American Games is a multi-sports event that includes athletics. It is open to athletes from North America, South America and the Caribbean. It was first hosted in 1951 in Argentina and is held once every four years. The 2007 competition saw some close competition with the women's discus throw decided by just 1 centimetre and the men's high jump by only 2 centimetres. Both winners were from Cuba, which is second in the all-time medal table behind the United States.

Buoban Pamang of Thailand gets into position to launch her gold medal winning throw at the South East Asian Games in 2005.

WORLD CHAMPIONSHIPS

The IAAF World Championships were first held in 1983. Since then it has become a massive event, second only to the Olympics in prestige. The IAAF also organises world championships for juniors, youths and an important indoor competition.

The World Championships

Initially held once every four years, from 1991 onwards, the World Championships have been held every two years, but never in an Olympic year. New events have been added, for example the women's triple jump in 1993 and the women's steeplechase in 2005. The World Championships take place over ten days. At the 2007 championships in Osaka, Japan, 1,978 athletes competed, while the 2009 competition in Berlin was watched live by more than half a million spectators.

STAT ATTACK

2007 World Championships Medal Table

Country	Gold	Silver	Bronze
1 USA	14	4	8
2 Kenya	5	3	5
3 Russia	4	9	3
4 Ethiopia	3	1	0
5 Germany	2	2	3
6 Czech Republic	2	1	0
7 Australia	2	0	0
8 Jamaica	1	6	3

Cuba's Alberto Juantorena competes in the discus as part of the men's decathlon at the 2007 World Championships. Juantorena is the son of the great runner of the same name – the only man to win the 400m and 800m Olympic titles.

In 2006 in Moscow, middle-distance-running legend Maria Mutola celebrated her seventh gold medal in the 800m at the World Indoor Championships.

Youths and Juniors

The IAAF runs two World Championships for aspiring athletes. The World Youth Championships is for athletes who are younger than 18 years old. Most events are similar to the adult championships, although the men's throwing events use a lighter discus, javelin, hammer and shot. At the first World Youth Championship, held in 1999, Yelena Isinbayeva and 400m hurdler Jana Pittman won events.

The World Junior Championships is open to 18 and 19 year olds, although sometimes younger athletes take part. IHeld once every two years, it first took place in 1986 when Javier Sotomayor won the high jump and Colin Jackson won the 110m hurdles. World Junior champions in 2002 included Carolina Klüft, Usain Bolt and Blanka Vlaši.

World Indoors

The indoor season runs through winter and early spring and, since 1985, a World Indoor Championships has been held every two years. One of the greatest achievements at this competition was Maria Mutola's dominance of the 800m. Between 1993 and 2006, she entered eight championships, winning gold at seven and silver in the other. She won bronze at the 2008 competition. At the same championship, Abubaker Kaki Khamis won the men's 800m for Sudan at the age of 18, while Russia's Yelena Soboleva broke the world indoor record in the 1500m.

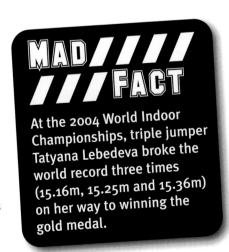

MAD FACT

At the 2004 World Indoor Championships, triple jumper Tatyana Lebedeva broke the world record three times (15.16m, 15.25m and 15.36m) on her way to winning the gold medal.

THE OLYMPICS

A revival of the Ancient Greek Olympic Games was first held in Athens in 1896. After uncertain beginnings, the Olympics has grown into the biggest sports event in the world.

Hosting the Games

Once every four years, the world's best athletes compete in the Summer Olympics. While other sports are highly popular during the two and a half weeks of competition, the athletics events are often the show-piece of the Games. The 4x400m relays tend to end Olympic action inside the main stadium, with the men's marathon often being the last gold medal event. Winning an Olympic event and receiving a gold medal is the pinnacle in athletics and the dream of most track and field athletes.

Athletics Events

There are 23 athletics events for women and 24 for men (the 50km racewalk is the extra event). The latest addition to the Olympics is the women's 3000m steeplechase, which debuted in 2008. This produced a world record, one of five world records and 17 Olympic records notched up at the 2008 Games, along with many scintillating performances by elite athletes such as Usain Bolt.

Carl Lewis wins the 100m final at the 1984 Olympics. He also won the 200m.

Who is...

...Carl Lewis?

Carl Lewis attended four Olympics and is the only track and field athlete in the modern era to win nine Olympic gold medals as well as a silver medal. Phenomenally fast, Lewis performed in the 100m and 200m sprints, and the 4x100m relay as well as the long jump. He gained a clean sweep of those events at his first Olympics in Los Angeles in 1984 and ended his long Olympic career in the United States at the Atlanta Games in 1996, winning gold in the long jump. Throughout his career, Lewis also won eight World Championship gold medals, making him one of the most successful and famous athletes in the world.

The Paralympics

Held shortly after the Olympics and at the same venues, the Paralympic Games are for elite athletes with a disability. The Paralympic Games has grown enormously from the 400 people that took part in Rome in 1960. Of the 4,200 plus competitors at the 2008 Paralympics, 1,035 took part in athletics events. Athletes are classified according to the type and severity of their disability – for example T11 is a class of visually-impaired track athletes, while athletes in F43 are amputees. Amongst the most popular events are wheelchair track racing, field athletic throwing events for those competitors confined to wheelchairs, and track running for blind or visually-impaired athletes. These athletes run alongside a sighted guide runner.

Wheelchair athlete Edith Hunkeler of Switzerland celebrates after winning the final of the women's marathon T54 event at the 2008 Paralympic Games.

ATHLETICS LEGENDS

Athletics has produced many great talents who have gone on to record amazing performances. Here are five legends of the sport.

MAD //// //// FACT

Natalya Lisovskaya's marriage to champion hammer thrower Yuriy Sedykh made them the only married couple to hold world records in field athletics.

Natalya Lisovskaya

Former Soviet athlete Lisovskaya dabbled with the discus but her main event was the shot put. In the mid-1980s, she kept on breaking her personal best as she won the 1985 and 1987 World Championships and the 1988 Olympics. Lisovskaya broke the world record three times, the last being in Moscow in 1987, where she threw 22.63m, a distance yet to be bettered.

Sergey Bubka

Ukranian Sergey Bubka redefined the pole vault with his power and gymnastic agility. He announced his arrival at the first World Championships in 1983 where he recorded a shock victory. Bubka went on to win the next five World Championships. In 1988 in Paris, he became the first person to successfully vault 6 metres. He went on to break the world outdoor record 17 times and win gold at the Olympics in 1988 and in 1994. His world record of 6.14m still stands.

Fanny Blankers-Koen

Blankers-Koen of the Netherlands was a 30-year-old mother of two by the time she reached the 1948 Olympics. Many people felt she was too old and should not compete. She responded by winning four golds (100m, 200m, 80m hurdles and the 4x100m). Blankers-Koen was voted by the IAAF as the 'Female Athlete of the Century' in 1999.

Fanny Blankers-Koen streaks ahead of her opponents in the 80m hurdles at the 1948 Olympics. She set or equalled 12 world records during her career.

42

Haile Gebrselassie

One of the finest long distance runners, Gebrselassie of Ethiopia won the 5,000m and 10,000m at the 1992 World Junior Championships. Two years later, he broke his first world record, smashing the best time for the 5000m by two seconds. In 1995, he destroyed the 5,000m world record by 10.9 seconds and the 10,000m world record by 9 seconds. He won gold in the 10,000m at the 1996 and 2000 Olympics, but since 2004 he has concentrated on marathon running, breaking the world record in 2008 by finishing in 2 hours, 3 minutes and 59 seconds.

MAD //// //// FACT

As a child, Haile Gebrselassie used to run 20km to school and back home again. He carried his books under one arm, and this led to his distinctive running style, in which he bends his left arm.

Michael Johnson

Blisteringly fast US athlete Michael Johnson blew away opponents in the 200m and 400m, winning five Olympic gold medals and nine golds at the World Championships. At the 1996 Olympics, Johnson, wearing gold shoes believed to weigh less than 100g, shredded the opposition with astonishing runs of 19.32 seconds in the 200m and 43.49 seconds in the 400m. In 2000 he became the first man to win the 400m Olympic title twice. In 1999, he cut the world record time for the 400m down to 43.18 seconds, a time that has yet to be beaten.

Michael Johnson roars triumphantly after his stunning win in the 200m final at the 1996 Olympics.

GLOSSARY

Amputee A person who has lost most or all of an arm or leg.

Anabolic steroids A type of banned substance in sport used by athletes to increase muscle size and strength.

Appearance fees Money paid to an athlete for taking part in a particular athletics meeting or competition.

Baton The short tube passed between relay runners in a race.

Cage The safety net and frame put up around the hammer and discus circles.

Changeover The exchange of the baton from one runner to the next in a relay.

Decathlon A men's combined event made up of individual track-and-field events. Athletes score points for their performances in each event.

Endurance The ability to continue doing a stressful activity for an extended period of time.

EPO Short for erythropoietin, a substance used by some athletes to increase endurance by illegally boosting the red blood cells that carry oxygen around the body.

False start When an athlete leaves the starting blocks before the gun has fired, or moves in the blocks and sets off the sensors.

Flexibility The physical ability to perform a full range of movements.

Grand Prix A type of major athletics meeting in which the competitors are professional athletes.

Heat A race in a preliminary round of an event. The top finishers in the heats advance to the next round.

Heptathlon The seven-discipline event for female athletes.

Landing sector The area in which a discus, javelin or shot put must land for the throw to count.

Pack The main group of runners in a middle- and long-distance race.

Paralympics An international competition for elite athletes with a disability.

Pentathlon A five-discipline event, usually for women, since replaced by the seven-event heptathlon.

Personal best   An athlete's best ever time, distance or height for an event.

Professional   To be paid and make a living by competing in athletics.

Replenish   To restore a body's supplies of liquid and nutrients.

Runway   The strip of track-like surface along which a javelin thrower, long jumper or triple jumper runs before throwing or jumping.

Scratch line   The line on the javelin runway which an athlete's foot must not cross.

Staggered start   Starting blocks placed in such a way to ensure that, when athletes run a race which includes a bend, each lane is the same length.

Stopboard   The wooden board at the front of a shot put circle.

Water jump   A pool of water up to 70cm deep that runners must cross on a steeplechase course.

Wind assistance   The strength of the wind blowing during certain running and jumping events, which can affect the times athletes may achieve.

World record   The best ever performance in an athletics event, which must be agreed upon by the IAAF (see websites column).

WEBSITES

WWW.IAAF.ORG

The website of the International Association of Athletics Federations is full of facts, news and a calendar of forthcoming athletics events.

WWW.OLYMPIC.ORG/UK/INDEX/UK.ASP

The website of the International Olympic Committee (IOC), which runs the Olympic Games. The website is packed with features, stories and results from past Games.

WWW.GBRATHLETICS.COM/IC/

This excellent athletics resource contains pages devoted to the results of major world championships along with world records and links to other athletics websites.

WWW.UKA.ORG.UK

The home page for United Kingdom Athletics, the organisation that runs athletics in Britain.

WWW.USATF.ORG

The official website of America's Track and Field team, this website contains athlete profiles as well as news and results of events.

WWW.PARALYMPICS.ORG.UK

This webpage leads to both the British Paralympic team and the parasport website which contains details of athletics and other Paralympic sports.

Note to parents and teachers:

Every effort has been made by the publishers to ensure that these websites are suitable for children, that they are of the highest educational value, and that they contain no inappropriate or offensive material. However, because of the nature of the Internet, it is impossible to guarantee that the contents of these sites will not be altered. We strongly advise that Internet access is supervised by a responsible adult.

INDEX